MW00592864

Learn to Make a
FOUNDATION-PIECED
Quilt™

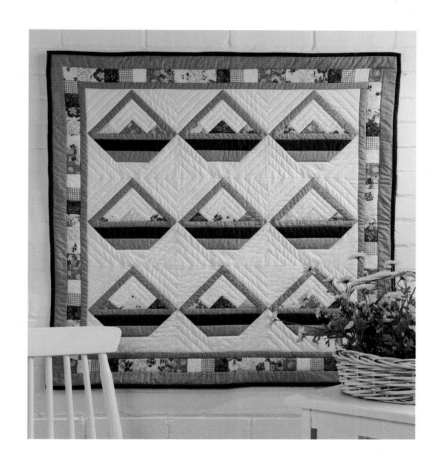

Annie's®

Introduction

Foundation piecing is a quiltmaking method that allows you to create magnificent quilts with exceptional accuracy and ease.

This progressive approach to patchwork frees you from the tedium of templates, careful cutting and meticulous measuring.

Follow our expert General Instructions to quickly learn the foundation-piecing technique, and then gather up your favorite, fabulous fabrics; then you'll be equipped and inspired to create your own quilt. Make any of the six distinctive quilts presented here, or venture on to other projects, with precise, uniform results—even when matching complicated points and seams.

Full-size foundation patterns for making the quilts in this book appear on pages 26–30.

Table of Contents

Fiber Optics,
page 20

Desert Trails,
page 16

General Instructions

Foundation piecing is the technique of sewing patchwork onto a foundation such as paper, fabric or stabilizer following a numerical sequence. The stitching lines are drawn, traced or transferred onto the foundation. The fabric pieces are placed on the unmarked side of the foundation, and then sewn from the marked side. Foundation piecing allows you to piece even the tiniest pieces accurately since all sewing follows drawn lines. This technique can be done either by machine or by hand, so you can take your blocks with you and stitch wherever you go.

Foundation Material

First, you must decide what type of foundation to use for piecing your blocks. There are several options. A light-color, lightweight cotton fabric and muslin are popular choices. Either fabric is see-through enough for tracing and will give your blocks extra stability. Of course, a fabric foundation adds another layer of fabric through which you will have to quilt. If you plan to hand-quilt, the extra thickness can make that quilting process a little more difficult.

Another choice for foundations is paper. For easy tracing, use any paper you can see through (notebook paper, copy paper, newsprint or computer paper), and then tear it away after sewing.

A third choice is tear-away stabilizer. Like muslin, it is light enough to see through for tracing, but like paper, it can be easily removed before quilting.

Preparing the Foundation

Tracing the Block

Trace the block pattern carefully onto your chosen foundation material. Use a ruler and a fine-point permanent marker to make straight lines and be sure to include all numbers. Draw a line ¼" from the outside edges of the block (Figure 1); cut along outside drawn line. Repeat for the number of blocks needed for your quilt.

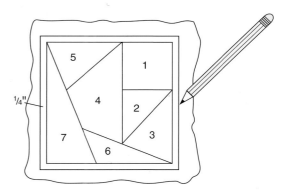

Figure 1

Mirror Images

Some of the blocks in this book are not symmetrical and when completed, they will appear as a mirror image of the pattern (Figure 2). You need to keep this in mind when deciding fabric placement.

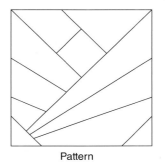
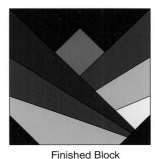

Pattern   Finished Block

Figure 2

Transferring the Block

The block patterns can also be transferred onto foundation material using a transfer pen or pencil. If your block is not symmetrical, trace the pattern onto tracing paper. Turn the paper over so the pattern is facedown (Figure 3 on page 4). You should still be able to see it clearly through the tracing paper; if not, use a light box or tape it to a sunny window. Trace the pattern onto the paper using a transfer pen or pencil. Then, following the manufacturer's directions, iron the transfer onto the foundation material. Write piece numbers on the foundation using a fine-point, permanent marking pen.

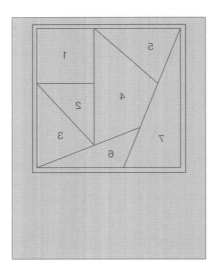

Figure 3

Note: If you do not trace the design onto tracing paper before using a transfer pen or pencil, your finished block will be a mirror image of the completed block as shown in Figure 2 on page 3.

Fabric

Use 100 percent cotton fabric for the blocks. All-cotton pieces stay in place better after finger pressing. If you must use a fabric other than 100 percent cotton, be sure to pin or glue each piece in place after each step.

Prewashing fabric is not necessary, but you must test your fabric to make certain it is colorfast and preshrunk (don't trust those manufacturers' labels). Start by cutting a 2"-wide strip (cut crosswise) of each fabric you have selected for your quilt. Measure both dimensions accurately for reference in the shrinkage test.

To determine whether fabric is colorfast, put each strip separately into a clean bowl of extremely hot water, or hold the fabric strip under hot running water. If fabric bleeds a great deal, all is not necessarily lost. You might just need to wash all of that fabric until all excess dye has washed out. Fabrics that continue to bleed after they have been washed several times should be eliminated.

To test for shrinkage, take each saturated strip and iron it dry with a hot iron. When the strip is completely dry, measure and compare it to your original measurements. If all your fabric strips shrink about the same amount, then it's really no problem. When you wash your finished quilt, you may achieve the puckered look of an antique quilt. If you do not

want this look, wash, dry and press all of your fabric before beginning so that shrinkage is no longer an issue. If only one of your fabrics is shrinking more than the others, it will have to be washed and dried, or discarded.

Carefully consider the design in both your fabric and your block before selecting and cutting your fabric and piecing your block. Hold the fabric at various angles and observe the effect on its pattern. Even uniform prints can change appearance when viewed lengthwise, crosswise and otherwise (Figure 4). Because the foundation-piecing method disregards grain line, you must plan ahead to achieve the desired effect.

 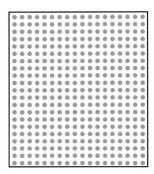

Figure 4

In some block designs, what appears as a single surface (usually the background) is comprised of several pieces; unless the pattern angles are aligned, the result could be unappealing (Figure 5). The best way to avoid this problem is to select fabrics with random prints.

 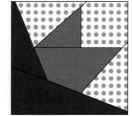

Figure 5

Cutting the Fabric

The advantage of foundation piecing is that you do *not* have to precisely cut every piece for every block. You can use strips, rectangles, squares or any odd-shaped scrap for piecing. You *do* have to be careful to use a piece of fabric that is at least ¼" larger on all sides than the space it is to cover. Triangle shapes can be a little tricky to piece. Use generous-size fabric pieces and be careful when positioning the pieces onto the foundation. You do waste some fabric this way, but the time it saves in cutting will be worth it in the end.

Making a Foundation-Pieced Block

1. Prepare foundations as described in Preparing the Foundation, page 3.

2. Turn foundation with unmarked side facing you and position fabric piece No. 1 right side up over the space marked No. 1 on the foundation. Hold foundation up to a light source to make sure fabric overlaps at least ¼" on all sides of space No. 1; pin or glue in place with a glue stick (Figure 6).

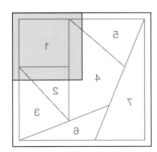

Figure 6

3. Place fabric piece No. 2 right sides together with piece No. 1. *Note: Double-check to see if fabric piece chosen will cover space No. 2 completely by folding it back over along line between spaces No. 1 and No. 2, (Figure 7).*

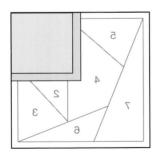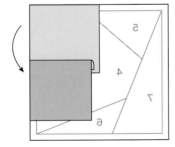

Figure 7

4. Turn foundation with marked side facing you and fold foundation forward along line between spaces No. 1 and No. 2; trim both pieces about ¼" above fold line (Figure 8).

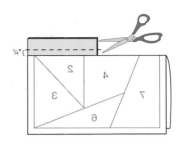

Figure 8

5. Open foundation out flat. With marked side of foundation still facing you and using a very short stitch length (to allow for easier paper removal), sew along line between spaces No. 1 and No. 2; begin and end sewing two to three stitches beyond line (Figure 9).

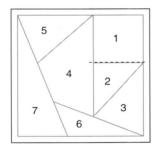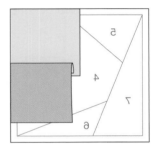

Figure 9   **Figure 10**

6. Turn foundation over. Open piece No. 2 and finger-press seam (Figure 10). Use a pin or glue stick to hold piece in place.

7. Turn foundation with marked side facing you; fold foundation forward along line between spaces No. 2 and No. 3 and trim piece No. 2 about ¼" from fold (Figure 11).

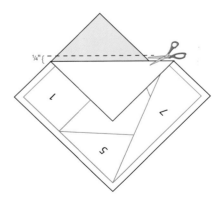

Figure 11

8. Turn foundation over and place piece No. 3 right side down even with just-trimmed edge, (Figure 12).

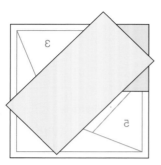

Figure 12

9. Turn foundation marked side up and sew along line between spaces No. 2 and No. 3; begin and end sewing two or three stitches beyond line (Figure 13).

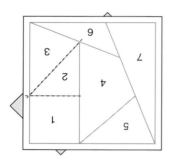

Figure 13

10. Turn foundation over, open piece No. 3 and finger-press seam (Figure 14). Glue or pin in place.

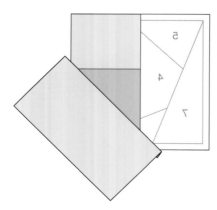

Figure 14

11. Turn foundation with marked side facing you; fold foundation forward along line between spaces No. 1, No. 2 and No. 4. If previous stitching makes it difficult to fold foundation forward, pull paper foundation away from fabric at stitching, and then fold along line. If using a fabric foundation, fold it forward as far as it will go and trim to about ¼" from drawn line (Figure 15).

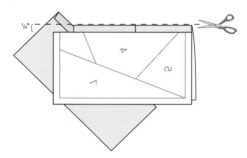

Figure 15

12. Continue sewing and trimming pieces in numerical order until block is complete. Press block, and then trim fabric even with outside line of foundation (Figure 16) to complete block (Figure 17). Do not remove paper or stabilizer at this time. It will stabilize the blocks as you sew them together since grain line was not always considered and many of the edges of the blocks can be stretchy, bias edges.

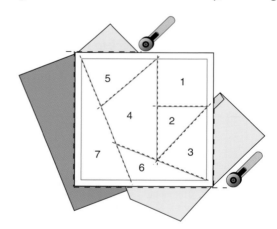

Figure 16

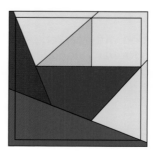

Figure 17

If you prefer to remove paper at this time, stay-stitch around entire block about ⅛" from edge (Figure 18).

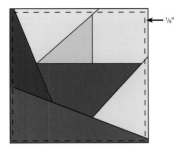

Figure 18

Making the Quilt Top

Sew the blocks together into pairs; press seams to one side, pressing adjacent seams in alternate directions (Figure 19).

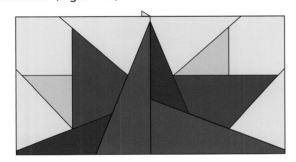

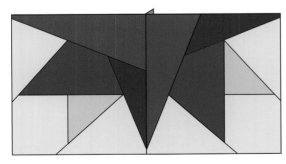

Figure 19

Sew pairs together, then pairs of pairs, until quilt top is completely sewn together (Figure 20).

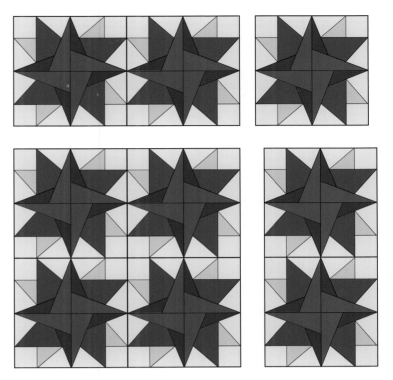

Figure 20

Adding Borders

Simple Borders

1. For simple borders, measure quilt top lengthwise; cut two border strips that length (Figure 21) and sew to sides of quilt.

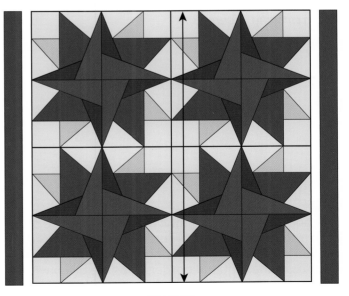

Figure 21

2. Measure quilt top crosswise, including borders just added, and cut two border strips that length (Figure 22). Sew to top and bottom of quilt top.

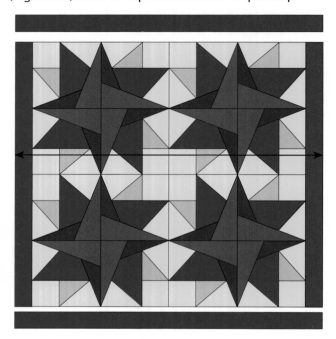

Figure 22

3. Repeat for any remaining borders.

Note: *If your fabric is not as wide (or long) as the border strips you need, you will have to piece the strips. It is always best to sew them together on the diagonal because it will be less noticeable. Trim excess fabric ¼" from stitching (Figure 23).*

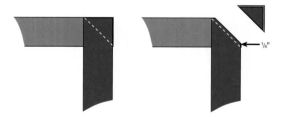

Figure 23

Pieced Borders

A good way to use up fabric pieces and finish a quilt top is to make pieced borders, such as those used in Radiant Rainbows and Spring Flower Baskets. The widths of the required border strips are given with the project instructions, while the lengths of the strips can vary, depending on size of fabric pieces or scraps.

1. Sew assorted strips together lengthwise; if lengths of strips vary, it is best to sew those closest in length next to each other (Figure 24). Press seam allowances to one side.

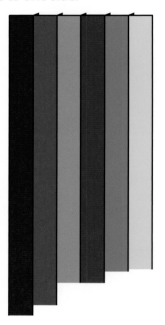

Figure 24

2. Cut across the strip sets at intervals equal to the original strip width (Figure 25). For example, if the strips were cut 1½" wide, you will cut at 1½" intervals.

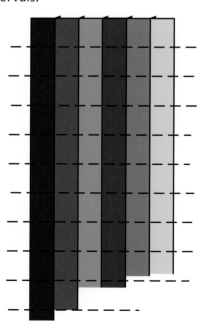

Figure 25

3. Sew pieced strips together end to end until necessary length is achieved (Figure 26). Repeat for another border strip.

Figure 26

4. Sew a border strip to each side of quilt top.

5. Measure quilt top crosswise (including borders just added). Repeat steps 1 to 3 for two strips and sew to top and bottom of quilt top (Figure 27).

Marking the Quilting Design

Note: If you have not yet removed the paper (or stablizer) foundation, do so at this time. Use a spray bottle of water to dampen paper for easier removal. Press quilt top carefully.

Before marking on your quilt top, be sure to test any marking material to make sure it will wash out of your fabric. Use a hard-lead pencil, chalk or special quilt-marking materials. If you quilt right on the marked lines, they will not show.

A word of caution: Marked lines, which are intended to disappear after quilting—either by exposure to air or with water—may become permanent when set with a hot iron. Therefore, don't iron your quilt top after you have marked your quilting pattern.

If you are quilting around shapes, you may not need to mark your line if you feel that you can accurately gauge the quilting line as you work. If you are quilting "in the ditch" of the seam (the space right in the seam), marking is not necessary. Other quilting lines will need to be marked.

If you plan to tie your quilt, you do not need to mark it.

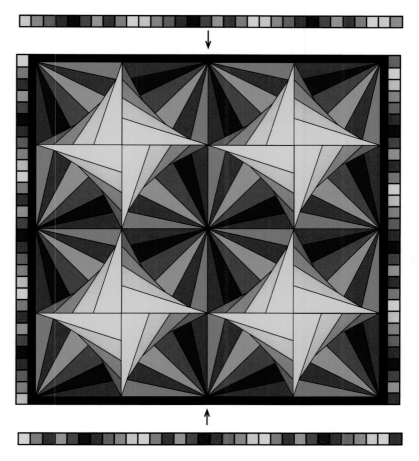

Figure 27

Attaching the Batting & Backing

There are a number of different types of batting on the market. Choose the one that is right for your quilt. Consider how the quilt will be used—will it be a bed quilt that will have to be washed periodically or will it be a wall hanging? Choose a batting type based upon use and type of quilting (hand or machine) following manufacturer's recommendations.

Note: Remove batting from its packaging a day in advance and open it out to full size. This will encourage the batting to lie flat.

Use 100 percent cotton fabric for the backing of your quilt. If your quilt top is wider than the most common fabric width (44"), you will most likely have to piece your backing fabric to fit the quilt top. Cut off the selvages and sew pieces together carefully; press seams open. Cut batting and backing about 3" larger than the quilt top on all sides. Place backing, wrong side up, on a flat surface. Place batting, centered, on top of backing, and then center quilt top right side up on batting (Figure 28).

Basting

The layers of the quilt must now be held together before quilting. There are three methods: thread basting, safety-pin basting and quilt-gun basting.

For thread basting, baste with long stitches, starting in the center and sewing toward the edges in a number of diagonal lines.

For safety-pin basting, pin through all layers at once, starting from the center and working out to the edges. Place the pins no more than 4" to 6" apart. Think of your quilt plan as you work and make certain that your pins avoid the prospective quilting lines. Choose size No. 1 or No. 2 rustproof safety pins.

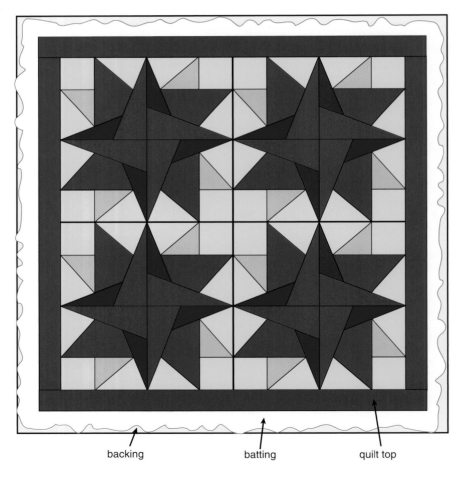

backing   batting   quilt top

Figure 28

For quilt-gun basting, use the handy trigger tool (found in quilt and fabric stores) that pushes nylon tags through all layers of the quilt. Start in the center and work randomly toward the outside edges. Place tags about 4" apart. You can sew right over the tags, and later, they can be removed easily by cutting them off with scissors.

Quilting

Your quilt may be either machine- or hand-quilted. *Note: Hand quilting may be a little more difficult if fabric or muslin was used as a foundation since there is an extra layer of fabric through which to quilt. If you have never used a sewing machine for quilting, you might want to read more about the technique. Check your local library or quilt fabric store or online for more information.*

You do not need a special machine for quilting. You can machine-quilt with almost any sewing machine. Just make sure it is oiled and in good working condition. An even-feed foot is recommended if you are going to machine-quilt since it is designed to feed the top and bottom layers of the quilt through the machine evenly.

Use fine, transparent nylon thread in the top and all-purpose sewing thread in the bobbin.

To quilt in the ditch (stitching in the space between two pieces of fabric that have been sewn together), use your fingers to pull the blocks or pieces apart and machine-stitch right between the two pieces. Try to keep your stitching just toward the side of the seam that does not have the bulk of the seam allowance under it. When you have finished stitching, the quilting will be practically hidden in the seam.

Free-form machine quilting is done with a darning foot and the feed dogs down on your sewing machine. It can be used to quilt around a design or to quilt a motif. Free-form machine quilting takes practice to master because you are controlling the quilt's movement through the machine rather than the machine moving the quilt. With free-form machine quilting, you can quilt in any direction—up and down, side to side and even in circles—without pivoting the quilt around the needle.

Attaching the Binding

Place the quilt on a flat surface and carefully trim the backing and batting ½" beyond the quilt-top edge. Measure the quilt top and cut two 2½"-wide binding strips the length of your quilt (for sides). Fold strips in half lengthwise, wrong sides together. Place one strip along one side of the quilt top, raw edges even; sew with a ¼" seam allowance (Figure 29). *Note: Seam allowance should be measured from outer edge of quilt-top fabric, not outer edge of batting/backing).*

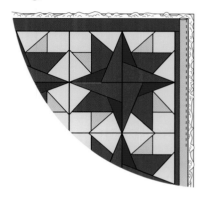

Figure 29

Turn binding to back and slipstitch to backing, covering previous stitching line (Figure 30). Repeat on other side.

Figure 30

For top and bottom edges, measure quilt crosswise, including side bindings just added, and cut two 2½"-wide strips that length, adding ½" to each end. Fold strips in half lengthwise with wrong sides together. Place one strip along top edge with ½" extending beyond each side; sew with a ¼" seam allowance (Figure 31). Turn binding to back and tuck the extra ½" under at each end; slipstitch to backing fabric.

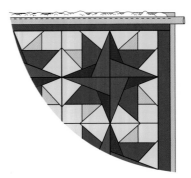

Figure 31

The Finishing Touch
When your quilt is finished, always sign and date it. A label can be cross-stitched, embroidered or even written with a permanent marking pen. Hand-stitch label to back of quilt.

Making a Larger Quilt
The quilts shown in this book are wall hangings. Most of the quilts are made up of four-block sections. One of the quilts, Spring Flower Baskets, page 24, uses the blocks set on point. To do this, sew a triangle (made by cutting two 6" squares in half diagonally) to each side of the block; the new block size is 9⅞" finished.

If you would like to make a bed-size quilt that looks like one of the wall hangings in this book, you will need to add blocks in multiples of two in each direction to maintain the design (Figure 32 on facing page).

Determine the size quilt you want by measuring the bed it will cover. If your quilt is intended for a bed that is not available for measuring, use the following guidelines:

Bed Size	Mattress Size
Crib	27" x 51"
Twin	39" x 75"
Double	54" x 75"
Queen	60" x 80"
King	76" x 80"

To the mattress measurements, add the drop (the part of the quilt that hangs over the edge of the mattress) and the tuck (the part that is tucked under the pillows). For example, if you want your quilt to hang 12" over the edge of the mattress with a 12" tuck, add 24" to the length and width of the mattress size.

The blocks in this book all have a finished size of 7" square. Therefore, you can use any of the blocks in your quilt, and they will fit together. Combine sashing and borders with the blocks to achieve the desired size.

Use the following chart as a guide in making a quilt to fit your bed. You may change border and sashing widths as desired.

Layout	Twin	Full/Queen	King
4" border	64" x 99" 8 x 13 104 blocks	78" x 99" 10 x 13 130 blocks	99" x 99" 13 x 13 169 blocks
2" sashing and 6" border	68" x 104" 6 x 10 60 blocks	86" x 104" 8 x 10 80 blocks	104" x 104" 10 x 10 100 blocks
grouped blocks with 3" sashing and 6" border border	66" x 100" 6 x 10 60 blocks	83" x 100" 8 x 10 80 blocks	100" x 100" 10 x 10 100 blocks
blocks with setting triangles, 3" border	65¼" x 104¾" 6 x 10 60 blocks	85" x 104¾" 8 x 10 80 blocks	104¾" x 104¾" 10 x 10 100 blocks
blocks with setting triangles, 3" sashing, 5" border	64½" x 103⅛" 4 x 7 28 blocks	90¼" x 103⅛" 6 x 7 42 blocks	103⅛" x 103⅛" 7 x 7 49 blocks

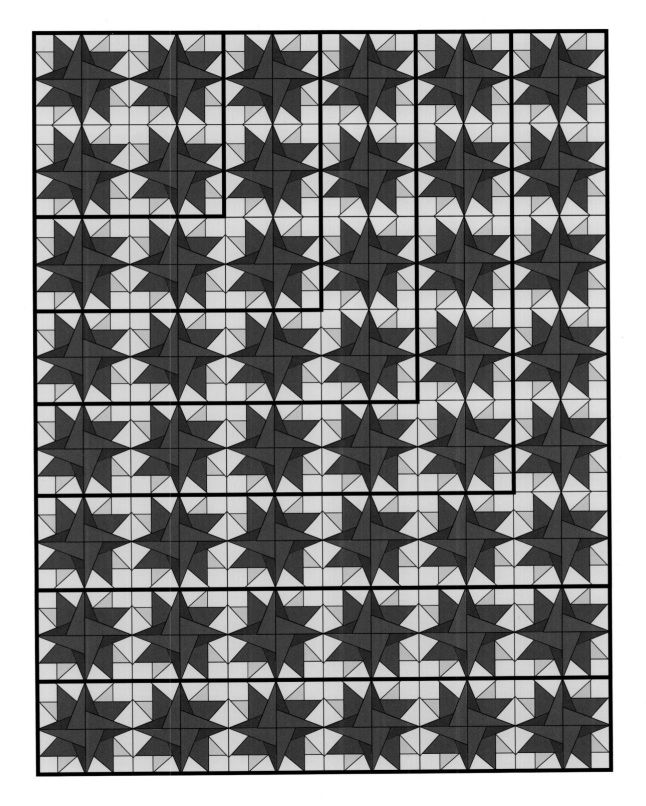

Figure 32

Starwinkle

Project Specifications
Quilt Size: 52" x 52"
Block Size: 7" x 7"
Number of blocks: 36

Materials
- 1¾ yards gold print, spaces No. 1, 3, 5 and second border
- ½ yard light periwinkle blue, space No. 2
- 1 yard medium periwinkle blue, space No. 4 and first border
- ¾ yard medium dark red print, space No. 7
- 1 yard dark red print, space No. 6 and third border
- ½ yard binding fabric
- Batting 58" x 58"
- Backing 58" x 58"
- Foundation material
- Neutral-color all-purpose thread
- Quilting thread
- Basic sewing tools and supplies

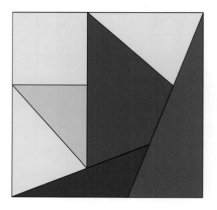

Star
7" x 7" Block
Make 36

Starwinkle
Placement Diagram 52" x 52"

Instructions
Note: *Read General Instructions, pages 3–13, before beginning.*

1. Referring to Tracing the Block, page 3, trace 36 block patterns (page 26) onto foundation material.

2. Beginning with space No. 1, sew fabric pieces to foundation in numerical order, referring to Making a Foundation-Pieced Block, pages 5–7. Repeat for a total of 36 blocks.

3. Referring to Placement Diagram, arrange blocks in six rows of six blocks each. Sew blocks together into pairs. Press seams for each row in opposite directions.

4. Sew pairs together, and then sew sections together. Press carefully. The quilt top should measure 42½" x 42½".

5. Cut the following border strips:
- two 1¾" x 42½" strips medium periwinkle (first border, sides)
- two 1¾" x 45" strips medium periwinkle (first border, top and bottom)
- two 1" x 45" strips gold (second border, sides)
- two 1" x 46" strips gold (second border, top and bottom)
- two 3½" x 46" strips dark red print (third border, sides)
- two 3½" x 52" strips dark red print (third border, top and bottom)

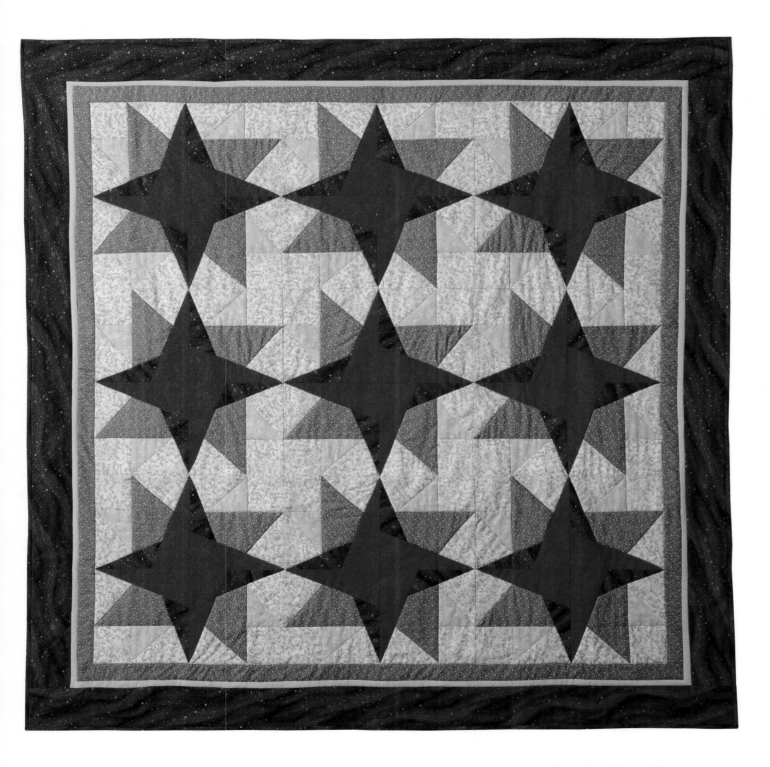

6. Add borders to quilt top, referring to Simple Borders, pages 7 and 8.

7. If you used a paper or stabilizer foundation, remove it carefully.

8. Layer, quilt and bind referring to General Instructions on pages 10 and 11. ❖

Desert Trails

Project Specifications
Quilt Size: 37" x 37"
Block Size: 7" x 7"
Number of Blocks: 16

Materials
- ⅛ yard each 4 yellow prints, spaces No. 1, 2, 7, 12, 17, 18 and 23
- ⅛ yard each 4 teal prints, spaces No. 1, 2, 7, 12, 17, 18 and 23
- ⅛ yard each 4 brown/rust prints, spaces No. 1, 2, 7, 12, 17, 18 and 23
- ⅛ yard each 4 green prints, spaces No. 1, 2, 7, 12, 17, 18 and 23
- ½ yard light ecru print, spaces No. 3, 8, 13, 14, 19 and 24
- ½ yard light medium ecru print, spaces No. 4, 9, 10, 15, 20 and 25
- ½ yard medium ecru print, spaces No. 5, 6, 11, 16, 21 and 22
- ⅜ yard brown dot for second border
- 1 yard teal floral for first border, third border and binding
- Batting 43" x 43"

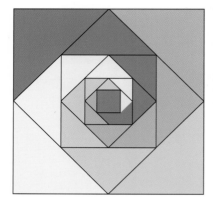

Snail
7" x 7" Block
Make 16

- Backing 43" x 43"
- Foundation material
- Neutral-color all-purpose thread
- Quilting thread
- Basic sewing tools and supplies

Instructions
Note: *Please read General Instructions, pages 3–13, before beginning.*

1. Referring to Tracing the Block, page 3, trace 16 block patterns (page 27) onto foundation material.

2. Beginning with space No. 1, sew fabric pieces to foundation in numerical order, referring to Making a Foundation-Pieced Block, pages 5–7. Repeat for a total of 16 blocks.

Note: *Referring to the Materials list above, write the fabric colors in the appropriate spaces on each foundation to make fabric placement easier.*

3. Referring to Placement Diagram, arrange blocks in four rows of four blocks each. Sew blocks together into pairs. Press seams for each row in opposite directions.

4. Sew pairs together, and then sew sections together. Press carefully. Quilt top should measure 28½" x 28½".

5. Cut the following border strips:
- two 1¼" x 28½" strips teal floral (first border, sides)
- two 1¼" x 30" strips teal floral (first border, top and bottom)

Desert Trails
Placement Diagram 37" x 37"

- two 2" x 30" strips brown dot print (second border, sides)
- two 2" x 33" strips brown dot print (second border, top and bottom)
- two 2½" x 33" strips teal floral (third border, sides)
- two 2½" x 37" strips teal floral (third border, top and bottom)

6. Add borders to quilt, referring to Simple Borders, pages 7 and 8.

7. If you used a paper or stabilizer foundation, remove it carefully.

8. Layer, quilt and bind referring to General Instructions on pages 10 and 11. ❖

Radiant Rainbows

Project Specifications
Quilt Size: 34½" x 34½"
Block Size: 7" x 7"
Number of Blocks: 16

Materials
- Fat quarter each of 10 rainbow colors
- ¾ yard black solid, first and third borders and binding
- Batting 41" x 41"
- Backing 41" x 41"
- Foundation material
- Neutral-color all-purpose thread
- Quilting thread
- Basic sewing tools and supplies

Instructions
Note: *Read General Directions, pages 3–13, before beginning.*

1. Referring to Tracing the Block, page 3, trace 16 block patterns (page 28) onto foundation material.

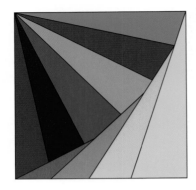

Rainbow
7" x 7" Block
Make 16

2. Beginning with space No. 1, sew fabric pieces onto foundation in numerical order, referring to Making a Foundation-Pieced Block, pages 5–7. Repeat for a total of 16 blocks.

3. Referring to Placement Diagram, arrange blocks in four rows of four blocks each. Sew blocks together in pairs. Press seams for each row in opposite directions.

4. Sew pairs together, and then sew sections together. Press carefully. Quilt top should measure 28½" x 28½".

5. Cut the following border strips:
- two 1½" x 28½" strips black solid (first border, sides)
- two 1½" x 30½" strips black solid (first border, top and bottom)
- several 1½"-wide strips assorted rainbow fabrics (second border)
- two 1½" x 32½" strips black solid (third border, sides)
- two 1½" x 34½" strips black solid (third border, top and bottom)

6. Referring to Simple Borders, pages 7 and 8, add first border to quilt top.

7. For second border, refer to Pieced Borders, pages 8 and 9. Sew strips together lengthwise; cut across sewn strips at 1½" intervals. For each side border, sew cut strips together to equal 30 squares; then sew a strip to each side of quilt top. For top and bottom borders, sew cut strips together to equal 32 squares; sew strips to quilt top.

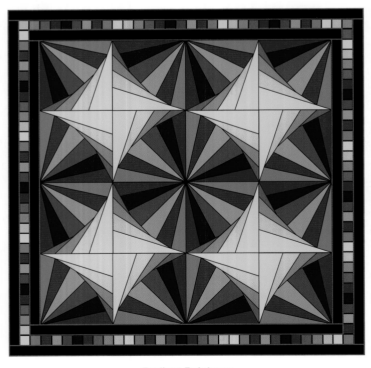

Radiant Rainbows
Placement Diagram 34½" x 34½"

8. Add third border as instructed in Simple Borders.

9. If you used a paper or stabilizer foundation, remove paper carefully.

10. Layer, quilt and bind referring to General Instructions on pages 10 and 11. ❖

Fiber Optics

Project Specifications
Quilt Size: 36" x 36"
Block Size: 7" x 7"
Number of Blocks: 16

Materials
- 1 yard black/blue print, spaces No. 2, 3, 10, 11, second border and binding
- ⅜ yard lavender tonal, space No. 6
- ⅝ yard pink dot, spaces No. 5 and 9
- ⅜ yard purple print, spaces No. 4 and 8
- ⅜ yard purple/blue batik, spaces No. 4 and 8
- ⅜ yard blue print, space No. 7
- ⅜ yard dark purple swirl, space No. 7
- ¼ yard dark pink print, space No. 1 and first border
- Batting 42" x 42"
- Backing 42" x 42"
- Foundation material
- Neutral-color all-purpose thread
- Quilting thread
- Basic sewing tools and supplies

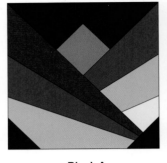

Block A
7" x 7" Block
Make 8

Block B
7" x 7" Block
Make 8

Instructions

Note: *Read General Instrucitons, pages 3–13, before beginning.*

1. Referring to Tracing the Block, page 3, trace 16 block patterns (page 29) onto foundation material.

2. For Block A, beginning with space No. 1, sew fabric pieces to foundation in numerical order, referring to Making a Foundation-Pieced Block, pages 5–7. ***Note:*** *Use purple print fabric for spaces No. 4 and 8 and use blue print fabric for space No. 7. Repeat for a total of 8 blocks.*

3. For Block B, beginning with space No. 1, sew fabric pieces to foundation in numerical order, referring to Making a Foundation-Pieced Block, pages 5–7. ***Note:*** *Use purple/blue batik fabric for spaces No. 4 and 8 and use dark purple swirl fabric for space No. 7. Repeat for a total of 8 blocks.*

4. Referring to Placement Diagram, arrange blocks in four rows of four blocks each alternating Blocks A and B. Sew blocks together in pairs. Press seams for each row in opposite directions.

5. Sew pairs together, and then sew sections together. Press carefully. Quilt top should measure 28½" x 28½".

6. Cut the following border strips:
- two 1¼" x 28½" strips dark pink print (first border, sides)
- two 1¼" x 30" strips dark pink print (first border, top and bottom)

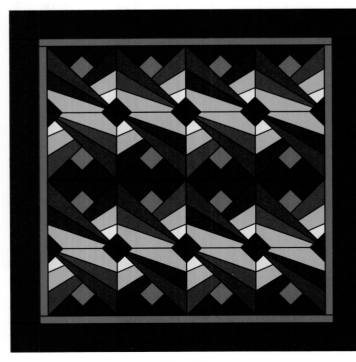

Fiber Optics
Placement Diagram 36" x 36"

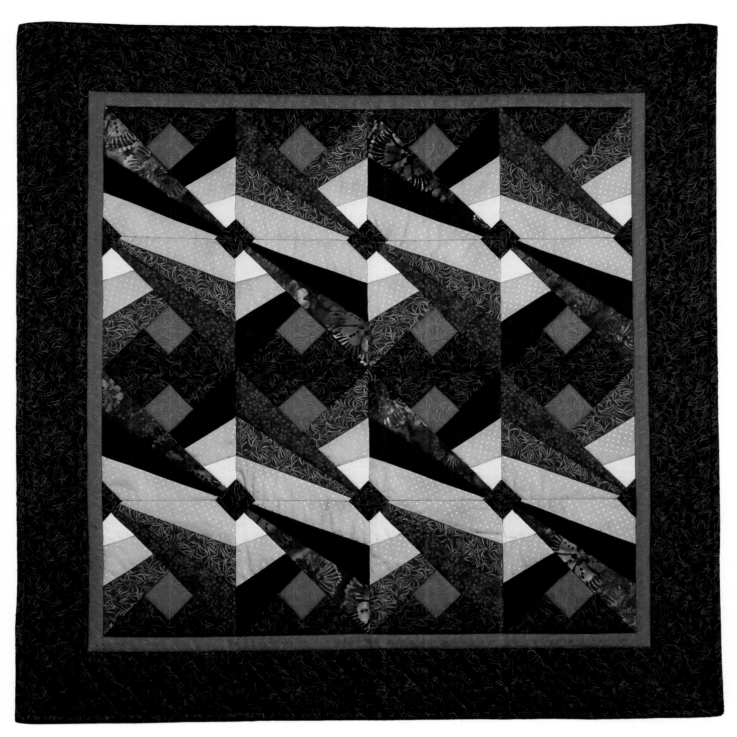

- two 3½" x 30" strips black/blue print (second border, sides)
- two 3½" x 36" strips black/blue print (second border, top and bottom)

7. Add borders to quilt, referring to Simple Borders, pages 7 and 8.

8. If you used a paper or stabilizer foundation, remove it carefully.

9. Layer, quilt and bind referring to General Instructions on pages 10 and 11. ❖

Santa Fe Baskets

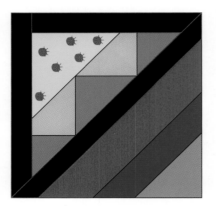

Basket
7" x 7" Block
Make 16

Project Specifications
Quilt Size: 36" x 36"
Block Size: 7" x 7"
Number of Blocks: 16

Materials
- 1 yard black print, spaces No. 7, 8 and 9
- ¼ yard tan/peach print, space No. 6 and second border
- ¼ yard peach, spaces No. 2 and 4
- ¼ yard turquoise solid, spaces No. 1, 3 and 5
- ½ yard coral, space No. 10 and first border
- ½ yard turquoise/black, space No. 11 and third border
- ¼ yard purple/tan, space No. 12
- ¼ yard binding fabric
- Batting 42" x 42"
- Backing 42" x 42"
- Foundation material
- Neutral-color all-purpose thread
- Quilting thread
- Basic sewing tools and supplies

Project Note
This quilt and the Spring Flower Baskets quilt (page 24) are made from the same foundation-pieced block pattern. The Spring Flower Basket quilt is assembled using triangles to set the blocks on point. This quilt is a straight-set version.

Instructions
Note: *Read General Instructions, pages 3–13, before beginning.*

1. Referring to Tracing the Block, page 3, trace 16 basket block patterns (page 30) onto foundation material.

2. Beginning with space No. 1, sew fabric pieces to foundation in numerical order, referring to Making a Foundation-Pieced Block, pages 5–7. Repeat for a total of 16 blocks.

3. Referring to Placement Diagram, arrange blocks in four rows of four blocks each. Sew blocks together into pairs. Press seams in opposite directions.

4. Sew pairs together, and then sew sections together. Press carefully. Quilt top should measure 28½" x 28½".

5. Cut the following border strips:
- two 1¾" x 28½" strips coral (first border, sides)
- two 1¾" x 31" strips coral (first border, top and bottom)

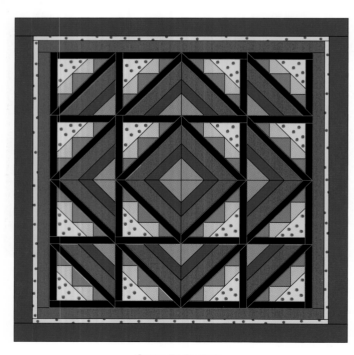

Santa Fe Baskets
Placement Diagram 36" x 36"

- two 1" x 31" strips tan/peach print (second border, sides)
- two 1" x 32" strips tan/peach print (second border, top and bottom)
- two 2½" x 32" strips turquoise/black (third border, sides)
- two 2½" x 36" strips turquoise/black (third border, top and bottom)

6. Add border strips to quilt top, referring to Simple Borders, pages 7 and 8.

7. If you used a paper or stabilizer foundation, remove it carefully.

8. Layer, quilt and bind referring to General Instructions on pages 10 and 11. ❖

Spring Flower Baskets

Project Specifications
Quilt Size: 38" x 38"
Block Size: 7" x 7"
Number of Blocks; 9

Materials
- 1¼ yards yellow, spaces No. 2, 4, 6, 12 and background triangles
- ¼ yard each of seven floral prints (or floral scraps), spaces No. 1, 3, 5 and second border
- 1¼ yards green print, spaces No. 7, 8, 9, 11, and first and third borders
- ½ yard dark green check, space No. 10 and binding
- Batting 44" x 44"
- Backing 44" x 44"
- Foundation material
- Neutral-color all-purpose thread
- Quilt thread
- Basic sewing tools and supplies

Project Note
This quilt and the Santa Fe Baskets quilt (page 22) are made from the same foundation-pieced block pattern. This quilt is assembled using triangles to set the blocks on point.

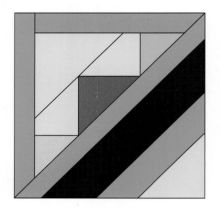

Basket
7" x 7" Block
Make 9

Instructions
Note: *Read General Instructions, pages 3–13, before beginning.*

1. Referring to Tracing the Block, page 3, trace nine block patterns (page 30) onto foundation material.

2. Beginning with space No. 1, sew fabric pieces to foundation in numerical order referring to Making a Foundation-Pieced Block, pages 5–7. Repeat for a total of nine blocks.

3. Cut 18 squares, 6" x 6", from yellow; cut in half diagonally. Sew a triangle to opposite sides of each block, and then to remaining sides. Figure 1.

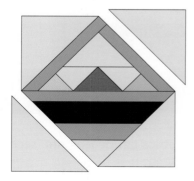

Figure 1

4. Referring to Placement Diagram, arrange blocks in three rows of three blocks each. Sew blocks together into rows. Press seams for each row in opposite directions.

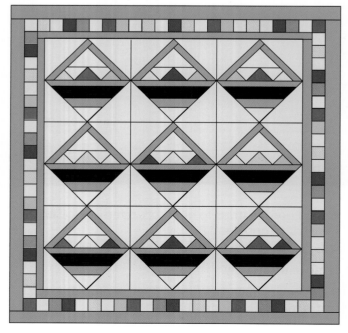

Spring Flower Baskets
Placement Diagram 38" x 38"

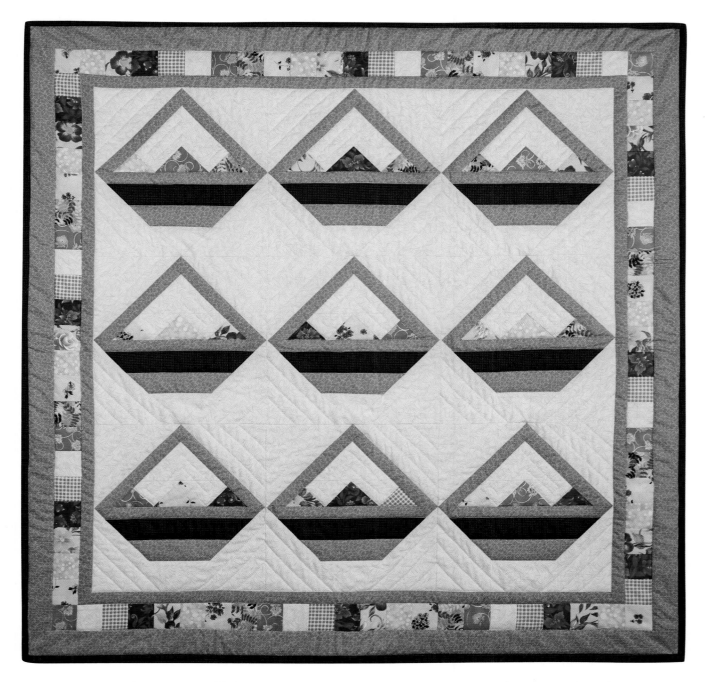

5. Sew rows together. Press carefully. Your quilt top should measure 30" x 30".

6. Cut the following border strips:
- two 1¼" x 30½" strips green print (first border, sides)
- two 1¼" x 32" strips green print (first border, top and bottom)
- several 2"-wide strips assorted floral prints (second border)
- two 2" x 35" strips green print (third border, sides)
- two 2" x 38" strips green print (third border, top and bottom)

7. Referring to Simple Borders, pages 7 and 8, add first border to quilt top.

8. For second border, refer to Pieced Borders, pages 8 and 9. Sew strips together lengthwise; cut across sewn strips at 2" intervals. For each side border, sew cut strips together to equal 21 squares; then, sew a strip to each side of quilt top. For top and bottom borders, sew cut strips together to equal 23 squares; sew strips to quilt top.

9. Add third border as instructed in Simple Borders.

10. If you used a paper or stabilizer foundation, remove carefully.

11. Layer, quilt and bind referring to General Instructions on pages 10 and 11. ❖

Starwinkle
Instructions on page 14

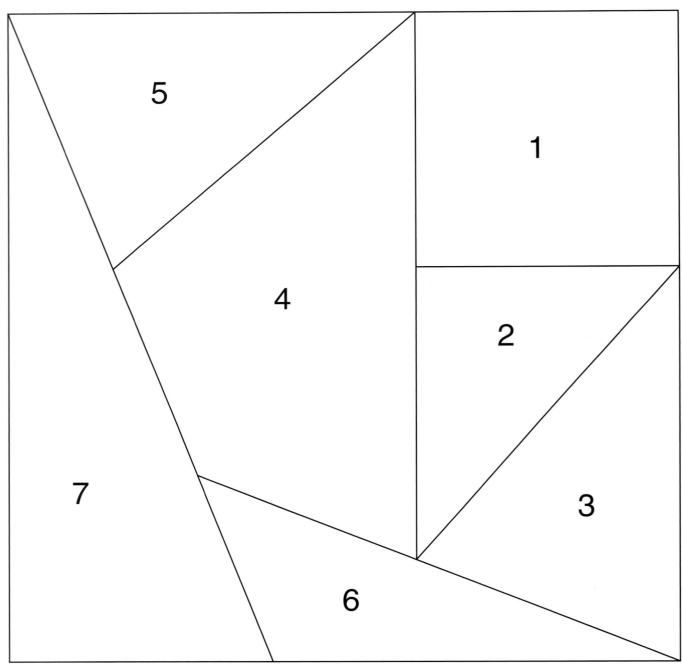

Starwinkle Block Pattern

Desert Trails
Instructions on page 16

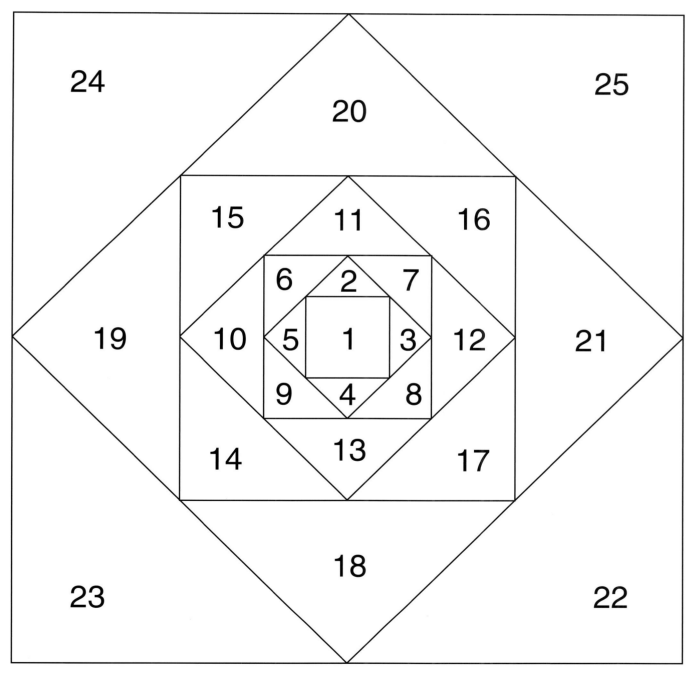

Desert Trails Block Pattern

Radiant Rainbows
Instructions on page 18

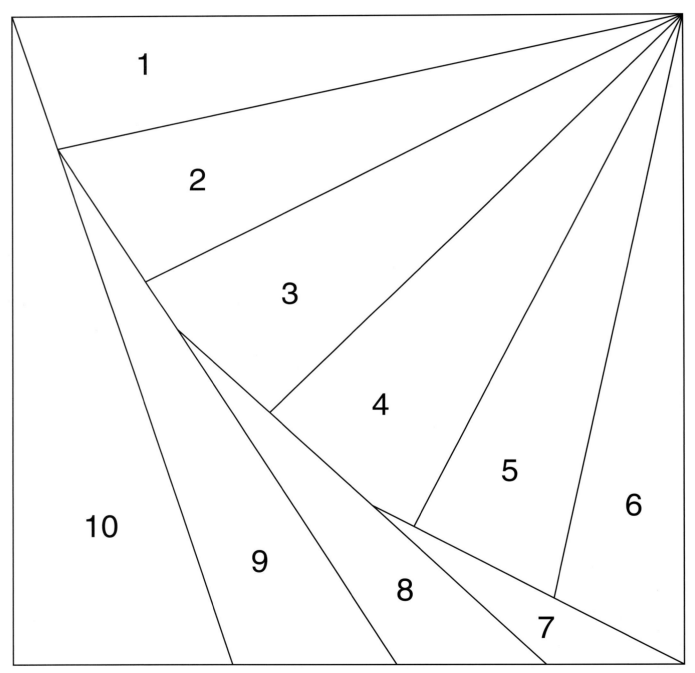

Radiant Rainbows Block Pattern

Fiber Optics
Instructions on page 20

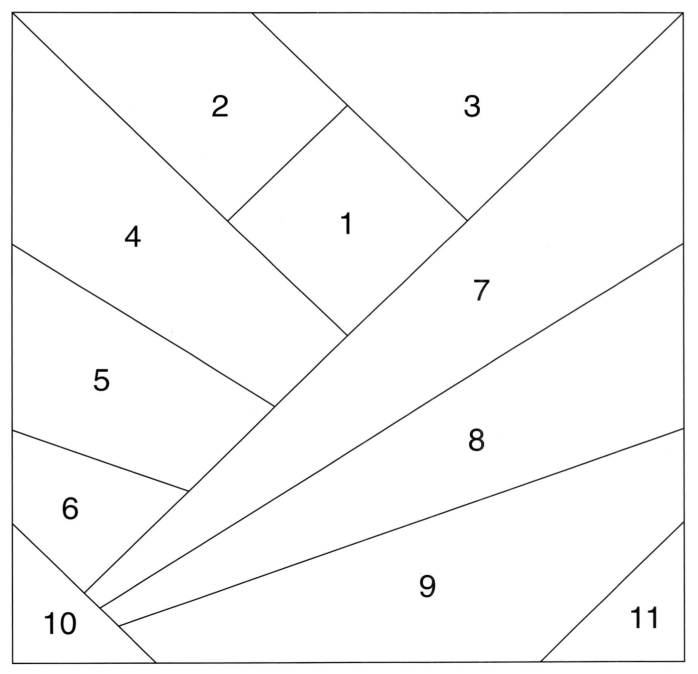

Fiber Optics Block Pattern

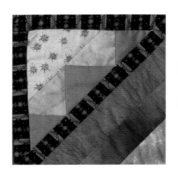

Santa Fe Baskets
Instructions on page 22

Spring Flower Baskets
Instructions on page 24

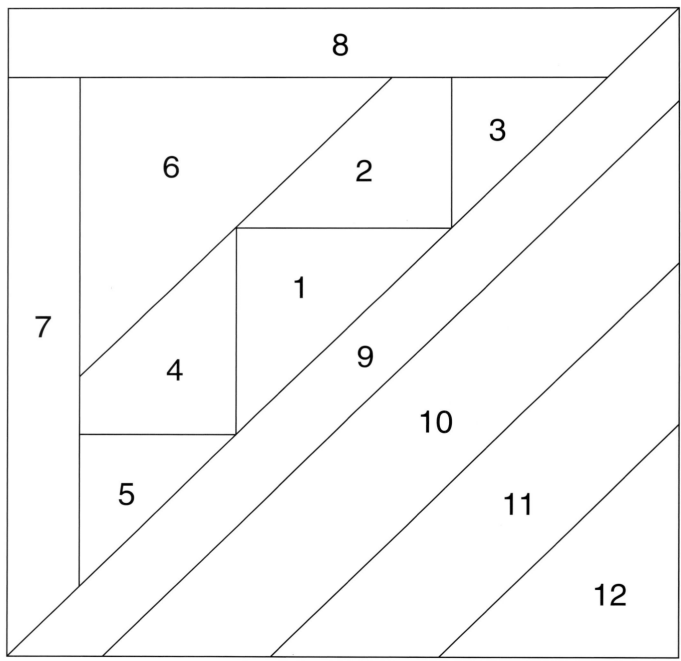

Basket Block Pattern

Metric Conversion Charts

Metric Conversions

Canada/U.S. Measurement		Multiplied by	Metric Measurement
yards	x	.9144	= metres (m)
yards	x	91.44	= centimetres (cm)
inches	x	2.54	= centimetres (cm)
inches	x	25.40	= millimetres (mm)
inches	x	.0254	= metres (m)

Canada/U.S. Measurement		Multiplied by	Metric Measurement
centimetres	x	.3937	= inches
metres	x	1.0936	= yards

Standard Equivalents

Canada/U.S. Measurement		Metric Measurement		
⅛ inch	=	3.20 mm	=	0.32 cm
¼ inch	=	6.35 mm	=	0.635 cm
⅜ inch	=	9.50 mm	=	0.95 cm
½ inch	=	12.70 mm	=	1.27 cm
⅝ inch	=	15.90 mm	=	1.59 cm
¾ inch	=	19.10 mm	=	1.91 cm
⅞ inch	=	22.20 mm	=	2.22 cm
1 inch	=	25.40 mm	=	2.54 cm
⅛ yard	=	11.43 cm	=	0.11 m
¼ yard	=	22.86 cm	=	0.23 m
⅜ yard	=	34.29 cm	=	0.34 m
½ yard	=	45.72 cm	=	0.46 m
⅝ yard	=	57.15 cm	=	0.57 m
¾ yard	=	68.58 cm	=	0.69 m
⅞ yard	=	80.00 cm	=	0.80 m
1 yard	=	91.44 cm	=	0.91 m
1⅛ yards	=	102.87 cm	=	1.03 m
1¼ yards	=	114.30 cm	=	1.14 m

Canada/U.S. Measurement		Metric Measurement		
1⅜ yards	=	125.73 cm	=	1.26 m
1½ yards	=	137.16 cm	=	1.37 m
1⅝ yards	=	148.59 cm	=	1.49 m
1¾ yards	=	160.02 cm	=	1.60 m
1⅞ yards	=	171.44 cm	=	1.71 m
2 yards	=	182.88 cm	=	1.83 m
2⅛ yards	=	194.31 cm	=	1.94 m
2¼ yards	=	205.74 cm	=	2.06 m
2⅜ yards	=	217.17 cm	=	2.17 m
2½ yards	=	228.60 cm	=	2.29 m
2⅝ yards	=	240.03 cm	=	2.40 m
2¾ yards	=	251.46 cm	=	2.51 m
2⅞ yards	=	262.88 cm	=	2.63 m
3 yards	=	274.32 cm	=	2.74 m
3⅛ yards	=	285.75 cm	=	2.86 m
3¼ yards	=	297.18 cm	=	2.97 m
3⅜ yards	=	308.61 cm	=	3.09 m
3½ yards	=	320.04 cm	=	3.20 m
3⅝ yards	=	331.47 cm	=	3.31 m
3¾ yards	=	342.90 cm	=	3.43 m
3⅞ yards	=	354.32 cm	=	3.54 m
4 yards	=	365.76 cm	=	3.66 m
4⅛ yards	=	377.19 cm	=	3.77 m
4¼ yards	=	388.62 cm	=	3.89 m
4⅜ yards	=	400.05 cm	=	4.00 m
4½ yards	=	411.48 cm	=	4.11 m
4⅝ yards	=	422.91 cm	=	4.23 m
4¾ yards	=	434.34 cm	=	4.34 m
4⅞ yards	=	445.76 cm	=	4.46 m
5 yards	=	457.20 cm	=	4.57 m

Published by Annie's, 306 East Parr Road, Berne, IN 46711. Printed in USA. Copyright © 2018 Annie's. All rights reserved. This publication may not be reproduced in part or in whole without written permission from the publisher.

RETAIL STORES: If you would like to carry this publication or any other Annie's publication, visit AnniesWSL.com.

Every effort has been made to ensure that the instructions in this publication are complete and accurate. We cannot, however, take responsibility for human error, typographical mistakes or variations in individual work. Please visit AnniesCustomerService.com to check for pattern updates.

ISBN: 978-1-59012-984-5

1 2 3 4 5 6 7 8 9

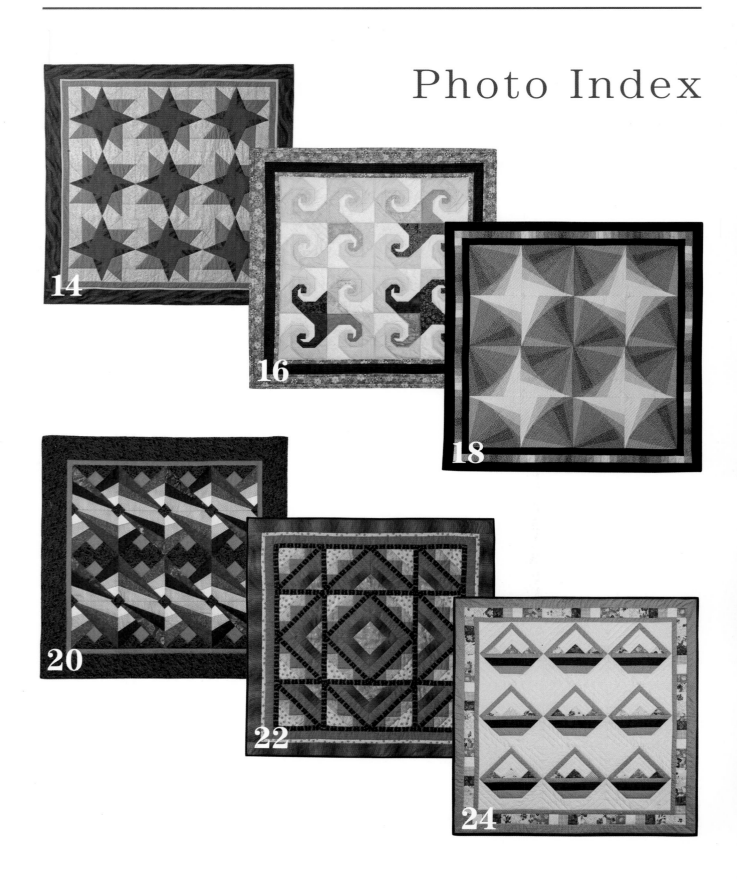